D1597850

Bye Bye the 'COVID -19'

"You can't catch us
We are stronger than you"

Information: MiLu Children's Educational Source. www.my-willing.com

ISBN: 978-1-64970-828-1

Bye Bye the 'COVID-19'

**"You can't catch us
Catch us, if you can"**

Grade 3 students said.

Yeah!

"Monday school will be reopened".

Mia is a grade 3 student.

She is counting with fingers.

"Today is Wednesday. Thursday, Friday, Saturday, and Sunday. Four days more for school reopen after the pandemic holiday.

I will meet my friends, classmates and teachers. I will play with my friends and classmates. I will learn new things at school". Mia said.

Monday morning Mia went to school. She met her friends, classmates and teachers. Mia and her friends were so happy to see each other.

In the group time, their teacher Maaree discussed with them about the holiday.

Lucas said, "We got the 'COVID-19' pandemic holiday".

The teacher said,

"Yes. Exactly Lucas.
We got the 'COVID-19' pandemic holiday because the 'COVID-19' is a new disease. It has not previously been identified in humans.

It can spread from person to person through close contact. Therefore, schools, daycares, and other people gathering places are closed and we got the pandemic holiday".

Mia said, "The 'COVID-19' is a Virus germ".

The teacher said,

"It's true Mia. There are four major types of germs: Bacteria, Virus, Fungus, and Protozoa. The 'COVID-19' is one of the Viruses".

Kayal said, "The germs are so tiny". The teacher said, "Yes. It's correct Kayal.

The germs are so tiny organisms. We can't see in normal eyes, but can see them through a microscope. When they get into our bodies, we don't know until we feel symptoms".

Kavin said, "The germs find in animals".

The teacher said,

"Ok, Kavin. The germs can find in animals. Also, they can find in people, plants, goods, air, soil, water, and food. They can find all over the world, in all kinds of places".

Nickol said, "A lot of people die by the COVID-19".

The teacher said,

"Yes, Nickol. A lot of people die by the 'COVID-19'.
Even though a lot of people have been recovering and become in normal life. Comparing with the recovering amount is much more than the death amount".

Zara said, "The 'COVID-19' is a killer".

The teacher said,

"Zara! Don't panic about this. Whoever feels fever, dry cough, shortness of breath, joint or muscle pain, sore throat, headache, chill, nausea, vomiting, diarrhea, lost sense of smell, and taste...

Contact to medical emergency.
Our wonderful health care workers provide medical treatment.
It helps to relieve symptoms".

Cheng said, "I am very scared about this".

The teacher said,

"Cheng! You don't scare about this.
We have a lot of help around us such as parents, relations,
neighbours, doctors, nurses, medical assistants, pharmacists,
personal support workers, social workers, and more.

Our excellent 'Frontline' workers can help us to prevent and
control spread of the 'COVID-19'.

They are 'Heroes' and doing extraordinary work for us.
They do hard works in the battle to win the COVID-19".

The teacher said,

"We have to support together to win the COVID-19".

Stay home as much as we can.

Maintain social distance at
least 2 meters length from others.

People who are living with you do not
need to distance from each other.

Away from crowded places.

Wear a mask when others around.
The face mask can block the
release of virus-filled droplets
from the nose and mouth with
others and us.

Keep distance for 14 days who
has symptoms and has arrived
from outside of the country.

Wearing gloves is important.
When touching shopping cart,
cash register, door handle, gas pump,
handling laundry, cleaning,
caring someone who is sick, and
when needed.

Avoid hands shake.
Hands can transport the viral
particles to the nose and mouth.

Only travel essential trips.

Kavin said, "Hands washing can kill the COVID-19".

The teacher said, "It's correct Kavin.
I am happy about your understanding of the way to kill the germs.

Proper hands washing is much protected from the 'COVID-19'.

Hands washing can keep us healthy.
Clean hands prevent the spread of germs
from one person to another.

Wash hands with clean running water and soap

- Wet hands and apply soap
- Lather and rub them at least 20 seconds, including the backs
  of hands, between fingers, and under nails. Then rinse hands well.
- Close the tap with paper towel.
- Dry hands with a clean towel or paper towel or air dry.

Use hand sanitizer

If soap and water are not available, use hand sanitizer.
Apply on the palm. Rub hands together on all surfaces include
back of the hands, between fingers, and under nails until dry".

These are the times must wash hands

Before and after eating food.

After handling garbage.

Before and after using the washroom.

Before, during, and after preparing food.

After sneezing, coughing and blowing the nose.

Before and after caring for the animal.

Before and after touching eyes, nose, and mouth.

After touching any dirty surface and objects.

After coming from the playground and outside.

Before and after treating the wound.

Before and after caring for someone who is sick.

Before and after changing a child's diaper, or helping toilet training.

Keep fingernails shorter

The germs can live underneath fingernails.

They are potentially contributing to the spread of the germs.

The teacher said,

"Our healthy habits help to win the COVID-19".

Mia said, "We have to clean our class room".

The teacher said,
"Correct Mia.
I appreciate your cleaning practice.
Cleaning practices help to control the
spread of infections.

Clean regularly household items, furniture, toys, toilets, phones, doors handles, TV, electronic devices, clothes, and more.
Also, classroom, playground, park, road, environment, and everywhere".

A clean environment is our part of the quality life.

Lucas said,

"When coughing, sneezing and blowing nose into facial tissue".

The teacher said,

"Yes, Lucas. I am very proud of your good habit.

This habit blocks the spread of infectious germs to others around them.

When coughing and sneezing, if the facial tissue is not available, use it in the upper sleeve or arm.

Dispose of used facial tissue as soon as possible in a closed waste bin.

 Afterward, wash hands or sanitize".

Proper garbage disposal prevents the spread of disease.

Lucas said, "Playing outside can prevent the COVID-19".
The teacher said, "It's true Lucas.

You said a great idea. It is a good practicing skill and improves the immune system with fun.

Outside playing is a good physical activity. Physical activities include playing, dancing, cycling, jogging, walking, yoga, and more.

Regular physical activity can improve our health.
Reduce the risk of several diseases.

When doing physical activities on the outside can get fresh air too.

Fresh air gives strength to the immune system.

Increasing the white blood cell function properly.

It's fighting and killing germs".

Nickol said, "Eating healthy food controls the COVID-19".

The teacher said, "Correct Nickol. It's a wonderful Message.

Nutritious and balanced foods provide our body and mind healthy.

Eat food with whole grains, low-fat meats, poultry, and milk products, fish, lentils, vegetables, fruits, nuts, seeds…

Drink a lot of water too. Water helps every system in the body functioning properly".

Lucas said, "Sleep can help to heal the COVID-19"

The teacher said, "Yes, Lucas. It's an amazing idea.

Sleeping is a very important part of people's mental and physical health.

It supports healing illness.

During the sleeping time, the body fights to prevent the infection.

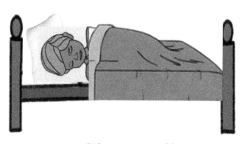

Also, the body restores and repairs various functions".

Sleep well

The teacher said,

"Save our natural resources and protect from the COVID-19".

Water, soil, air, sun, trees, animals and more are our natural resources. These are essential to survival for our life.

They help to heal and prevent several illnesses".

Zara said, "We need to love with animals".

The teacher said, "Marvelous idea Zara. I am very happy to hear from you.

Animals are closely associated with humans' in daily life.

They serve food, cloth, fertilize, and much more for us.

Some animals are our pets. They make us feel happy.

Only touch animals if needed".

Love and care animals.

Cheng said, "Trees keep to our environment healthier".
The teacher said
"Exactly correct Cheng. I pleased to hear from you.

Trees help to give cleaner air, water, and soil.
Trees provide food, medicine, furniture, shade and more.
They offer shelter for birds and creatures.

Keep plants healthier

Make sure plenty of space to grow.
Plants need equal sunlight everywhere.
Watering plants in the proper amount.

Plants can use sunlight to make their own food.
Provide fertilizer for extra nutrients to grow plants healthily".

Plant trees and make a green world.

Kayal said, "It is our responsibility to save water".
The teacher said, "Exactly correct Kayal.
Your message makes me pleased.

The water relates to the essential purpose in humans, plants, and animals to live.

We use water to drink, clean, preparing food, watering plants, produce electricity, and more.

Save the water

Tightly turn off the faucet when not in use.

Turn off the tap when brushing teeth, soaping hands and face.

Bath for a shorter duration.

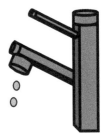

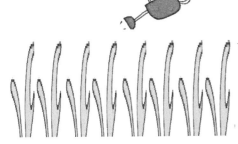

Water the plants in the morning or evening.

Collect rainwater and use it for the plants.

Use recycle water when possible".

Nickol said, "Use to speaking in a soft voice".

The teacher said,

"It's correct Nickol. I am very proud of your best way of speaking.

Soft sound reduces headache, anxiety, fear, helps to sleep, increases concentration, and more.

Maintain the sound

Talk in a soft voice inside the place.
Raise hand, take a turn, and talk.
Listen and focus when others talk.

Take deep breaths and do relax.
Stay calm, close eyes, listen to
the sound and feel the smell.

Turn down the sound volume and
listen to the soft sound.

Practice it a habit to walk.
Ride in the bicycle.
Travel by public transportation is better.

Grow plants.
The stems, leaves, branches, and
all part of the tree absorb sound waves".

Mia said, "My mom uses reusable bags for shopping".

The teacher said, "It's a great job, Mia's mom does.

Reusable bags reduce environmental pollution.

The use of reusable bags help to keep soil, water, air, trees, animals and humans healthier.

Use fabric, paper, hemp bag.
Use paper bag for waste".

Cheng said, "My mom tells me to use loose parts for creative".

The teacher said,
"Cheng's mom tells a good idea.

Use loose parts, recycle materials, and natural things for creative.

It helps to develop creative skills and connects to the environment clean".

The environment is a relationship with the human's health and well-being.

The teacher said,

"Getting social support can increase strength to win from COVID-19".

Zara said, "Be friends with others".

The teacher said, "Yes, Zara. I am very pleased about Zara's friendly manner.

Friendship increases our sense of belonging, happiness, self-confidence, reduces illness and more.

Play with same age group children.

You get something or help from others say thank you.

Use please word end of your requests.

When you make mistakes, say sorry.
Use positive words, talk, laugh, and have fun.

Share whatever you can such as books, toys...
Whoever struggle help them".

Kayal said,

"My dad tells me to help anyone in need".

The teacher said,

"Yes, Kayal. I appreciate your dad's advice.

If you feel who are suffering, go close,
talk, and help them".

Helping is making happiness to others and
feeling happy for us.

Kavin said, "We have to respect people equally".

The teacher said, "It's right Kavin. I am very glad to get from you.

It gives of esteem, happiness,
confidence, safety, reduces
fear, sickness and more.

Everyone has different knowledge,
skills, experiences and abilities.

Speak kindly and politely.
When you are doing teamwork respects other's ideas.
Encourage whoever to do their best.
Praise persons' abilities, and achievements".

Respecting is one of the most important qualities we have.

The teacher said,

"The scientists are researching and analyzing for the healing of the COVID-19".

Mia said,

"The vaccination successfully controls the COVID-19"

The teacher said,

"Yes, Mia. I am proud of your knowledgeable thinking.

They will invent vaccination and medicine for it in the future.

The vaccination and the medicine will help for win the 'COVID-19'.

The vaccination to help the immune system develops and protects from the 'COVID-19'.

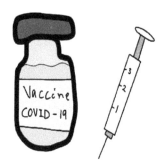

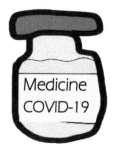

The medicine can cure the 'COVID-19' caused by a virus".

"We all have to practice in healthy habits for protecting from COVID -19"

Grade 3 students and teacher Maaree said.

Yeah!

"We do a wonderful job of challenging with the COVID-19".

Hooray!!!!!!!
We win from 'COVID-19'

Bye Bye the 'COVID-19'

"You can't catch us any more.
We all follow the healthy habits.
We are stronger than you".

Grade 3 students said.

Printed in the USA
CPSIA information can be obtained
at www.ICGtesting.com
LVHW062116240224
772740LV00024B/1493